Strategic Studies Institute
and
U.S. Army War College Press

REGIONALIZING EAST MEDITERRANEAN GAS:
ENERGY SECURITY, STABILITY,
AND THE U.S. ROLE

Laura El-Katiri
Mohammed El-Katiri

December 2014

*****

Comments pertaining to this report are invited and should be forwarded to: Director, Strategic Studies Institute and U.S. Army War College Press, U.S. Army War College, 47 Ashburn Drive, Carlisle, PA 17013-5010.

*****

This manuscript was funded by the U.S. Army War College External Research Associates Program. Information on this program is available on our website, *www.StrategicStudies Institute.army.mil*, at the Opportunities tab.

*****

*****

The Strategic Studies Institute and U.S. Army War College Press publishes a monthly email newsletter to update the national security community on the research of our analysts, recent and forthcoming publications, and upcoming conferences sponsored by the Institute. Each newsletter also provides a strategic commentary by one of our research analysts. If you are interested in receiving this newsletter, please subscribe on the SSI website at *www.StrategicStudiesInstitute.army.mil/newsletter*.

FOREWORD

In recent years the distribution of the world's exploitable energy reserves has shifted markedly. One major change is the discovery of substantial gas deposits offshore the Levant. But while these deposits have the potential to revolutionize the economies of the net energy importers, Cyprus, Lebanon, and Israel, they also bring into sharp focus long-running disputes over maritime boundaries and sovereignty. In short, these deposits provide yet another cause for conflict in an already deeply troubled region.

This monograph explores both the positive and negative implications of the Eastern Mediterranean's new gas reserves for the region, and the implications of both for U.S. interests. It combines the recognized expertise of two researchers with long experience in regional and energy studies, respectively. Their conclusion is that the management of these new energy resources is likely to influence significantly the relationships among the states in the region, particularly between Israel and its neighbors, including the Palestinian Territories.

The Strategic Studies Institute therefore recommends this monograph not only for its direct relevance to energy studies, but also to policymakers working with the broader issues of the Levant and Eastern Mediterranean as a whole.

DOUGLAS C. LOVELACE, JR.
Director
Strategic Studies Institute and
    U.S. Army War College Press

ABOUT THE AUTHORS

LAURA EL-KATIRI is a London-based academic who formerly taught at the Department of Financial and Management Studies at the School of Oriental African Studies, University of London. Her primary research is in oil markets and energy policy, with special focus on the Middle East and North Africa. Ms. El-Katiri has published widely on issues including oil and development in the Arab world, natural resource wealth in resource-rich economies, domestic energy market and pricing reform, and energy poverty; she has followed the East Mediterranean region's energy development for many years.

MOHAMMED EL-KATIRI is a Director of MENA Insight, a political risk consultancy that focuses on the Middle East and North Africa, and a Senior Research Analyst at the United Kingdom's (UK) Conflict Studies Research Centre (CSRC). Before joining CSRC, Dr. El-Katiri was a Research Fellow at the UK Defence Academy, and later served as a Political Risk Analyst at Eurasia Group and as a Senior Researcher at the Hague Institute for Global Justice. With more than 10 years of regional experience, Dr. El-Katiri focuses his research interests on political and economic security in North Africa and the Gulf Cooperation Council (GCC) states, as well as on North African relations with the European Union and security policies around the Mediterranean. Dr. El-Katiri has published numerous internal and external UK Defence Academy reports, including reference papers on national and regional security issues in the GCC and the Mediterranean, and a monograph on the Algerian national oil and gas company, Sonatrach. In addition, his publications include commentaries and research papers in a range of languages for research organizations in the UK and Europe, as well as various newspaper articles in and about the region. Dr. El-Katiri is a frequent media commentator, including for the British Broadcasting Company, the *Financial Times*, and *Al-Jazeera*.

SUMMARY

The East Mediterranean has been witnessing an unparalleled natural resource boom since the late-2000s, when Israel, followed by Cyprus, made its first significant offshore hydrocarbon discoveries in many years. These discoveries have since proven to be substantially larger than any other resources previously explored in the East Mediterranean Sea. A 2010 U.S. Geological Survey suggests the Levant basin—the area including Cyprus and Israel's offshore zones, and the offshore and some onshore territories of Syria, Lebanon, and the Palestinian Territories—could hold as many as 1.7 billion barrels of oil and up to 122 trillion cubic feet (tcf) of natural gas, leaving as much as two thirds of the region's potential resource base still undiscovered.

The East Mediterranean's newly discovered and potential future hydrocarbon resources are of tremendous economic and geostrategic significance, not only for the region itself but also for its main allies, including the United States. Economically, emerging gas producers Israel and Cyprus stand to gain considerably from their newly discovered gas wealth, which provides both a cost-effective source of energy for their historically import-dependent energy economies and a potential high-value source of revenues from gas exports into and beyond the region. Geostrategically, the presence of hydrocarbon resources in the East Mediterranean opens a great deal of opportunity for closer regional cooperation, but it also raises the potential for conflict over these valuable resources. The region also hosts two of the world's most intractable border conflicts: the Arab-Israeli conflict, involving territorial disputes between Israel, the Palestinians, Lebanon, and Syria, and the unresolved Cypriot question, leading to disputed boundaries on land and at sea and disputed ownership over hydrocarbon resources between the Greek- and Turkish-Cypriot communities.

This shifting energy landscape in the East Mediterranean is thus also significant for the region's main political and military partnerships. Israel, Cyprus, and Turkey are key strategic U.S. allies. Neighboring Egypt, Syria and Lebanon play important roles from the European and U.S. perspective, both as direct neighbors to Israel and the Palestinian Territories as well as because of their strategically important location as the geographic interconnection between Europe, North Africa, and the Middle East. Regional and extra-regional military alliances could be put under tension as a result of shifting geopolitical weight and relations between the key regional players, as well as the risk of re-emerging boundary conflicts following discoveries of subsea hydrocarbon resources. There is the potential for considerable policy dilemmas for the United States, if its local security partners find themselves having a confrontation over hydrocarbon resources and maritime boundaries.

This monograph provides an overview of recent hydrocarbon discoveries and their significance for the region's resource holders; it also explores the possible implications of these resources for the region's security landscape, their potential to fuel conflict, and options to foster closer regional cooperation and trade integration. It discusses the role U.S. diplomacy and military support could play to ensure continued stability, security, and regional support within the East Mediterranean's shifting geoeconomic framework.

REGIONALIZING EAST MEDITERRANEAN GAS: ENERGY SECURITY, STABILITY, AND THE U.S. ROLE

INTRODUCTION

The East Mediterranean has been witnessing an unparalleled natural resource boom since the late-2000s, when Israel, followed by Cyprus, made its first significant offshore hydrocarbon discoveries in many years. These discoveries have since proven to be substantially larger than any other resources previously explored in the East Mediterranean Sea. At the time of this writing, they consist primarily of natural gas, although liquids are expected to be discovered offshore as well, including in the potentially hydrocarbon-rich waters of Lebanon and Syria. A 2010 U.S. Geological Survey suggests the Levant basin — the area including Cyprus and Israel's offshore zones, and the offshore and some onshore territories of Syria, Lebanon, and the Palestinian Territories — could hold as much as 1.7 billion barrels of oil and up to 122 trillion cubic feet (tcf) of natural gas, leaving as much as two-thirds of the region's potential resource base still undiscovered.[1]

The East Mediterranean's newly discovered and potential future hydrocarbon resources are of tremendous economic and geostrategic significance not only for the region itself but also for its main allies, including the United States. Economically, emerging gas producers Israel and Cyprus stand to gain considerably from their newly discovered gas wealth, which provides both a cost-effective source of energy for their historically import-dependent energy economies, and a potential high-value source of revenues from gas exports into and beyond the region.

1

Geostrategically, the presence of hydrocarbon resources in the East Mediterranean opens a great deal of opportunity for closer regional cooperation, but it also raises the potential for conflict over these valuable resources. The region also hosts two of the world's most intractable border conflicts: the Arab-Israeli conflict, involving territorial disputes between Israel, the Palestinians, Lebanon, and Syria, and the unresolved Cypriot question, leading to disputes over boundaries on land and at sea, and disputes of the ownership over hydrocarbon resources, between the Greek- and Turkish-Cypriot communities.

This shifting energy landscape in the East Mediterranean is also significant for the region's main political and military allies. Israel, Cyprus, and Turkey are key strategic U.S. allies. Neighboring Egypt, Syria, and Lebanon play important roles from the European and U.S. perspective, both as direct neighbors to Israel and the Palestinian Territories as well as because of their strategically important location as the geographic interconnection between Europe, North Africa, and the Middle East. Regional and extra-regional military alliances could be put under tension as a result of shifting geopolitical weight and relations between key regional players, as well as the risk of re-emerging boundary conflicts following discoveries of subsea hydrocarbon resources. There is the potential for considerable policy dilemmas for the United States, if its local security partners find themselves in conflict over hydrocarbon resources and maritime boundaries.

This monograph will explore the strategic consequences of recent natural gas discoveries for the East Mediterranean security landscape, through the lens of U.S. security interests in the region. It first provides an overview of recent hydrocarbon discoveries and their significance for the region's resource holders; this is followed by an exploration of the possible implications of these resources for the region's security landscape, their potential to fuel conflict, and options to foster closer regional cooperation and trade integration. We then look at the role U.S. diplomacy and military support could play to ensure continued stability, security, and regional support within the East Mediterranean's shifting geoeconomic framework.

BACKGROUND: A BRIEF SUMMARY OF EAST MEDITERRANEAN HYDROCARBON DEVELOPMENTS IN THE 2000s

The East Mediterranean has been a relatively slow starter in terms of offshore exploratory activities. With most exploration work focused on less challenging on-land territory, much of the Levant appeared to be the Middle East's only remaining hydrocarbon-poor province. With the exception of Syria, which had been the only regional producer of significant oil and natural gas for several decades,[2] the remainder of the East Mediterranean was, as a result, a net-importing region, with Israelis, Cypriots, Lebanese, and Palestinians having long depended on imports for virtually their entire domestic energy needs.[3] The recent discoveries offshore Israel and Cyprus will completely change this picture: similar prospects for Lebanon and, potentially, the Palestinians could emerge if similar commercially viable hydrocarbon deposits materialize in their own territorial waters.

Israel's Breakthrough Discoveries.

Israel has one of the East Mediterranean's most extensive exploration histories, reaching back as far as the 1950s. As direct consequence of the Arab-Israeli conflict and Israel's resulting isolation among its Arab neighbors, there was strong historical interest in any means of increasing the country's energy self-sufficiency, and thereby in reducing Israel's exposure to supply risks via trade embargos and the interruption of trade routes by land and sea.[4] While it soon became apparent that the Levant — the small strip of land extending from Syria in the North down southward to the Gaza Strip — would be no second Arabian Peninsula in terms of hydrocarbon resources, Israeli exploration efforts were rewarded in 1998-99 with the small, but nevertheless significant, discovery of the Noa and Mari-B fields just off the Israeli coastline.[5] The two fields were comparably small, but with 1.5-tcf of reserves, Mari-B proved large enough to make production commercially viable and to contribute toward Israel's domestic gas supply by the mid-2000s.[6] Mari-B has been in operation since 2004, and together with Noa, remains until today Israel's only producing gas fields, covering around 60 percent of the country's natural gas demand.[7]

The picture of some isolated, small Israeli gas finds changed significantly during the late-2000s, however. Owing to consistent further exploration efforts, Israel was able to report a series of commercial gas discoveries starting in 2009, with the discovery of the 9.7-tcf Tamar field by a consortium led by U.S. Noble in cooperation with several smaller Israeli companies.[8] This large (by East Mediterranean standards) exploration success was further topped by the 2010 discovery of

4

the 19-tcf Leviathan field close to the maritime boundary with Cyprus, which has so far remained one of the largest single discoveries in the entire offshore Mediterranean.[9] Discoveries followed of smaller fields: Sara (1.47-tcf) and Dalit (350-530 million cubic feet), both in 2009, Myra (4.24-tcf) in 2010, and further fields thereafter.[10] While most of Israel's natural gas discoveries have yet to translate into proven gas reserves, in 2013 Israel held a total of 9.48-tcf of proven and 30-tcf estimated reserves, positioning Israel ahead of all East Mediterranean countries in terms of gas reserves and resource prospectivity.[11]

Cypriot Gas.

Cyprus, bordering the geographical structure that since the early-2000s has been believed to hold substantial hydrocarbon potential, began its own offshore exploration program during that decade. With historically no hydrocarbon reserves, and as a geographical island state, Cyprus has had few energy options and has relied on oil imports for its entire energy needs.[12] Rising prices of oil on international markets since 2002 and the country's growing financial difficulties since the late-2000s have given additional political impetus to the island's own natural resource exploration program. Cypriot efforts were rewarded in 2011 with the discovery of significant hydrocarbon deposits in its most southeasterly economic zone in Block 12, with an estimated resource base of between 3- and 9-tcf.[13] Cyprus has since tendered out four more offshore blocks, which have been signed up for by consortia led by European majors ENI and Total, and is planning for another licensing round in late-2014-15.[14]

Other East Mediterranean possibilities: Syria, Lebanon, and the Palestinian Territories.

Israel and Cyprus's exploration successes sparked substantial interest in neighboring countries as well. Syria, the most experienced gas producer in the East Mediterranean, followed Israel's initial discoveries in 1998 with exploration efforts in its own offshore territories, though the priority given to onshore production reduced the pace at which these efforts were pursued. An exception to the East Mediterranean's lack of historical oil and gas reserves, Syria already holds small, but essentially proven, oil and natural gas reserves of 2.5 oil barrels (bbl) and 8.5-tcf respectively, allowing Syria energy self-sufficiency for most of its modern history as well as moderately sized exports of oil to Turkey and Europe, currently disrupted due to civil war in the country.[15]

In May 2007, the Syrian government launched a first offshore bidding round, which ended with no rewards despite modest initial investor interest. This resulted from a combination of discouraging factors for international investors, including geopolitical and cost-benefit deterrents.[16] A second bidding round in early-2012 had to be cancelled due to the gradual deterioration of domestic stability following the outbreak of civil protests and infighting as the political upheavals of the Arab Spring began to sweep into Syria in early-2011.[17] Syria's descent into civil war has since prevented any re-emergence of offshore exploration efforts, while the series of international sanctions that has followed various atrocities in the continuing conflict makes foreign investment in the sector nearly impossible at the time of this writing.[18] Once the Syria conflict is resolved, prospects for Syrian offshore production — provided commercial resources are found — are high; Syria's existing experience as a producer of both oil and gas should help the country develop any potential offshore resources relatively smoothly once the political situation allows for any new exploration efforts in its offshore territories.

Another interested neighbor with substantial geological prospects for offshore hydrocarbons is Lebanon. Lebanon's exploration work commenced during the 2000s, followed (after much haggling over political posts) by the institutionalization of exploration licensing, with the creation of a Petroleum Authority in December 2012 and the launch of the country's first bidding round in February 2013.[19] Political stalemate in the absence of a parliament with decisionmaking powers has since delayed the finalization of the legal framework for an award of exploration and production licenses, and resolution appears remote at the time of this writing.[20] The election of a new stable government in Lebanon able to resolve the current climate of political stalemate is likely to speed up the award of licenses and the exploration of Lebanon's offshore territory — currently stated by the Lebanese government to hold potential for as much as another 30-tcf of natural gas as well as some 660 million barrels of oil.[21]

Similar to the remainder of the East Mediterranean, the Palestinian offshore territories near Gaza are believed to hold substantial hydrocarbon potential. Exploration in Palestinian waters was, in fact, already taking place during the 1990s, with two discoveries announced by an operating consortium led by BG from the United Kingdom in 2000 off the coast of Gaza. Control over Gaza's offshore territories had been relinquished in 1999 by Israel to the Palestinian Authority (PA), rendering the development of these offshore discoveries in principle a Palestinian matter.[22] A development plan for the 30 billion cubic meters (bcm) (1-tcf) Gaza Marine field stumbled, however, after obstruction by Israel over concerns regarding the flow of revenues to Palestinian stakeholders, leaving the development of these resources unaddressed until today.[23]

EAST MEDITERRANEAN HYDROCARBON RESOURCES AND REGIONAL CONFLICT POTENTIAL

The East Mediterranean has been a political flashpoint for much of its 20th- and 21st-century history. The region encompasses two of the world's most intractable political conflicts, the Arab-Israeli conflict, fought out in several wars and in continued political conflict between Lebanon, Syria, Israel, and political opposition groups in both the Palestinian Territories and other neighboring countries, and the still unresolved Cyprus conflict, drawing in neighboring Turkey. Both Israel and Cyprus are key U.S. allies and pillars of U.S. foreign policy in the region: Israel, with its long history of close political ties with the United States, historically has stood at the heart of American efforts to secure regional peace; while Cyprus forms the most eastern part of Europe and is an important strategic location for both U.S. and British military interests. East Mediterranean gas may complicate relations still further in this already geopolitically fragile region, placing efforts to encourage regional cooperation at the center of any desirable policy response.

The Arab-Israeli Conflict.

Arab-Israeli relations have held the Levant region back from any fruitful economic cooperation for more than half a century, and are likely to continue to affect progress in the East Mediterranean's offshore resource development. In fact, the presence of valuable natural resources in disputed territory may further feed the conflict. Continued conflict between Israelis and Palestinians over land and settling rights, and a series of wars fought between Israel and several of its Arab neighbors, have led to severely strained relations between the two sides. Military action between Israel and Gaza is ongoing, with the latest armed confrontation between Israel and Hamas since July 2014 serving as a painful reminder of the continued volatility of Israeli-Palestinian relations. Diplomatc relations between Israel on the one hand, and Lebanon and Syria on the other, remain nonexistent, with the two sides still de facto at war.

The potentially enormous economic value of hydrocarbon discoveries for the region's current and prospective producers raises the stakes, and furthermore, provides an additional high-value target in any future armed conflict between the various sides.[24] The Bank of Israel projects an overall positive effect of natural gas production on the country's balance of payments of around $3.5 billion (bn) in 2014, and has announced plans to purchase foreign currency during 2015. The same projections suggest the natural gas industry may contribute around 1 percent to the gross domestic product (GDP) for 2013 (worth some $22 bn) and 0.7 percent in 2014.[25] Other East Mediterranean countries attach similar high values to the development of their yet-to-be-explored offshore hydrocarbon resources;

some Lebanese government estimates have placed the value of Lebanon's unconfirmed hydrocarbon riches at between U.S.$300 bn and U.S.$700 bn, around seven times the country's current GDP, and a transformative factor for Lebanon's economy, which has been in disarray for many years.[26]

In the past, natural gas development and trade have more than once fallen hostage to the region's geopolitical difficulties. One of the most direct consequences of strained Israeli-Palestinian relations has been the lack of development of offshore gas resources discovered offshore Gaza in the late-1990s, despite the obvious economic benefits this development would have offered to the infant Palestinian economy.[27] Israel has blocked any development of the resources since 2000 over concerns regarding the channeling of Palestinian gas revenues into alleged terror finance, supposedly funding armed attacks against the State of Israel. A 4-year development plan for Gaza's offshore resources approved by the PA has since been discarded, while a breakdown in negotiations with Israel has driven lead developer BG and its partnering companies effectively to abandon Palestinian waters despite the resources' prospectivity.[28]

Continuing regional tensions give rise to concern over both the security situation within Israel and the stability of Israeli borders, not only with the Palestinian Territories but with other, neighboring Arab countries. Following the fall of the Hosni Mubarak regime in Egypt and subsequent political turmoil, Egypt's main gas pipeline to Israel and Jordan became subject to recurring rebel attacks targeting the Egyptian government and aimed at cutting gas export revenues.[29] After more than a year of unstable Egyptian gas supplies, in April 2012 Israel faced the cancellation of its existing gas supply contract by the newly elected Muslim Brotherhood government, which deprived Israel of its primary source of natural gas imports.[30] Israel's domestic power sector was effectively saved by the country's recent discoveries of its own resources, and the rapid start of production from the offshore Tamar field largely compensated for the natural gas deficit resulting from the cutoff of Egyptian supplies.[31] But the evident vulnerability of Israel to disruption of energy supplies from its Arab neighbors undoubtedly has strengthened the political lobbies within Israel that oppose any export of Israeli hydrocarbon resources at all.[32] These lobbies consider Israel's hydrocarbon resources more of a sovereignty asset than a mere commercial commodity.

Israel's political isolation within the Arab world also affects the range of companies willing to invest there. This is of particular significance in the context of liquefied natural gas (LNG) technology, which will have to be acquired from the small range of international companies with the relevant know-how. The continued weight of Arab oil and gas producers as critically important partners for major international oil companies (IOCs) means that investment decisions involving Israel are especially sensitive. Fear of sanctions by Arab countries against IOCs and service companies operating in Israel may deter otherwise interested companies from entering the Israeli market. Similarly, Cyprus may experience similar consequences with respect to companies with significant exposure in Turkey, although the scope of these repercussions is likely to be smaller than in the case of Israel, given the relatively smaller number of international companies operating in Turkey as opposed to the Arab world as a whole.

The future development of offshore hydrocarbon resources in Israel and Lebanon's sea waters could face still further complications, due to the two countries' rival claims over both onshore and offshore maritime territory. Israel's decision in early-2013 to grants exploration licenses for the Syrian-claimed Golan Heights spells potential for another armed conflict between the two parties should substantial hydrocarbon resources be discovered.[33] While Syria's current domestic situation may to a certain extent reduce the probability of any impeding conflict in the short term, a more immediate potential conflict area awaits farther along Israel's maritime boundaries. Lebanese-Israeli borders remain only informally demarcated, and follow the 2000 Blue Line with unresolved border disputes both on land and offshore. Lebanese and Israeli claims over maritime territory overlap over an area of around 850 square kilometers (km)—not a large area by international standards, but one over which neither country appears willing to compromise.[34] None of Israel's confirmed discoveries so far fall into the disputed area, but Lebanon's 2013 licensing round included bidding options for one out of three possible exploration blocks on the Lebanese side that crosses Israel's claimed maritime boundary.[35]

Against a history of previous war and military intervention between Israel and Lebanon, mutual threats of using military force to protect the integrity of what each side considers its exclusive economic zone reach back to 2010, when the issue first emerged in both parties' news media; Israeli Infrastructure Minister Uzi Landau (the Ministry of Infrastructure, remaining at the time of this writing the relevant ministry for Israel's hydrocarbon developments), for instance, commented in June 2010:

We will not hesitate to use our force and strength to protect not only the rule of law but the international maritime law. . . . Whatever we find, they [Lebanon's parliament and political circles] will have something to say. That's because they're not challenging our findings and so-called occupation of the sea. Our very existence here is a matter of occupation for them. These areas are within the economic waters of Israel.[36]

These remarks followed previous statements made by Lebanese Energy Minister Gebran Basil that Lebanon "will not allow Israel or any company working for Israeli interests to take any amount of our gas that is falling in our [exclusive economic] zone."[37]

Meanwhile, the dispute also has delayed the delimitation of the Cypriot-Lebanese and Cypriot-Israeli exclusive economic maritime zones, despite Cypriot efforts to mediate in its own right between the two parties.[38] In the case of an armed conflict between Israel and Lebanon, the security of the wider Levant region could once again be at stake, with a possible escalation of the conflict into neighboring Syria and the Palestinian Territories, as well as (with historical precedents) Jordan and Egypt. In combination, the pre-existing political problems in all of these countries—Syria destabilizing into de facto civil war, Egypt in the midst of political instability, the Palestinians and Lebanese lacking stable political cores—the potential for a new, escalating regional war is a threatening scenario indeed. Offshore hydrocarbon development plans along the East Mediterranean coast would immediately be impacted, as a high-profile target for military and terrorist attacks. Not least for this reason, both Israel and Lebanon face serious concerns over the desirability of potential future LNG liquefaction plants along their crowded and densely inhabited coastlines, as well as the vulnerability of as-yet-unbuilt gas pipelines across both countries and, possibly onward, to neighboring countries.[39] Cyprus, too, could be affected, given the geographic proximity between Israel's largest gas field, Leviathan—a potential site for Israeli gas production facilities—and Cyprus's gas field where production is expected first, Block 12. Wider regional conflict could also affect Egypt's significantly larger offshore gas production, further escalating the extent of potential disruptions caused by Israeli-Lebanese conflicts over gas resources.

The Cypriot Knot.

On the other side of the East Mediterranean shore, another decades-old conflict holds similar potential for re-escalation into armed conflict in case of unresolved rivaling claims over territorial waters and their potential hydrocarbon riches. Cyprus has been the site of confrontation among different interests for most of its modern history. Greek and Turkish Cypriots continue to inhabit the island state divided into the Greek-dominated South and the Turkish-dominated North. The Republic of Cyprus, which on paper comprises the whole island, is internationally recognized and a member of the EU, while the Turkish communities in the North of the island declare themselves a separate state, recognized only by Turkey.[40] This division of the island state has led to rivaling claims by both groups over land and maritime territory, and now over the allocation of potential export revenues from offshore gas reserves. While the Government of the Republic of Cyprus has assured that Cyprus's gas-export revenues would benefit all Cypriots once a comprehensive peace agreement has been settled, the absence of any such agreement, or indeed, of prospects for the conclusion of a comprehensive peace any time in the near future, raise questions over how Cyprus's two communities will accommodate the expected inflow of revenues once Cypriot gas leaves Cyprus's planned export facilities. This is also pertinent in view of previous propositions to use Cyprus's hydrocarbon wealth as collateral for current and future national borrowing.[41]

Turkish-Cypriot claims have been supported on the political level by Cyprus's key ally, Turkey, which has warned Nicosia to suspend development of any offshore reserves until the Cypriot question is eventually settled; Turkey, in fact, called the start of Cypriot exploration activities a "provocative and irresponsible" act[42] and stated that it would do "whatever necessary" to defend Turkish and Turkish-Cypriot rights.[43] A further statement followed issuance of Cyprus's second offshore tender round in February 2012 that Turkey would "take all necessary measures to protect its rights and interests in the maritime areas falling within its continental shelf."[44] International Crisis Group observers report complaints by Greek Cypriots over Turkish harassment inside Cyprus's maritime zone, where Turkey has reportedly carried out military exercises, approaching within five nautical miles of installations — described by Greek-Cypriot observers as "gunboat diplomacy."[45]

In the absence of a comprehensive settlement, Turkey and the Turkish-Cypriot community signed an agreement delineating their continental shelf in September 2011, assigning exploration licenses for seven offshore blocks, six of them in Greek-Cypriot areas (Blocks 1, 2, 3, 8, 9, and 13).[46] The Turkish state oil company *Türkiye Petrolleri Anonim Ortaklığı* (TPAO) reportedly has since begun to explore for hydrocarbon resources inside the Turkish-Cypriot-claimed territories,[47] despite (at the time of this writing) no apparent confrontation over exploration efforts with consortia operating in Nicosia's tendered-out license blocks. Potential for future conflict over offshore territories also results from direct Turkish maritime claims, which overlap with some of Nicosia's demarcated offshore blocks in the southwest. The four blocks in question formed part of the package of blocks on offer for licensing in the country's last licensing round in 2012, but, despite reporting bids, ended up not being licensed out.[48] It is more likely, however, that Cyprus will end up tendering out the respective blocks in question at a future bidding round, raising a parallel question to the Israeli-Lebanese water dispute as to how the different parties involved would react to a substantial hydrocarbon discovery in the disputed blocks.

Any suspension of the development of Cyprus's offshore resources would likely alarm not only the Cypriot government, but many of Cyprus's main political and economic allies as well. Cyprus, bailed out by an International Monetary Fund (IMF) and EU-backed rescue loan of $10 bn in March 2013 but still on the edge of economic bankruptcy, has already begun to build part of its future economic recovery plans on the growth of an indigenous natural gas industry and on the expected revenue from the export of natural gas from its offshore territories.[49] Politically caused delays in this development would likely exacerbate the normal delays resulting from potentially disappointing geologic and field performance (as has been the case following Cyprus's second appraisal drilling in October 2013).[50] This would further complicate the country's already precarious financial situation.

An armed conflict between the two Cypriot communities, possibly involving Turkey, would place yet another military conflict at the periphery of the EU, threatening the stability of the EU's most eastern border and its political and commercial relations with Turkey. Continued deadlock over the Cypriot question, contributed to by disputes over offshore hydrocarbon reserves, would also continue to hamper the ability of North Atlantic Treaty Organization (NATO) partners to cooperate more closely with Cyprus, given NATO member Turkey's continued resistance to strategic NATO cooperation. Cyprus's geostrategic location between West Asia and Eurasia, on the other hand, renders Cyprus a highly desirable NATO partner, as well as a strategic partner for the United States, which maintains strategically important military facilities there. Escalating conflict between Cyprus and Turkey may also further feed into existing political instabilities across the East and Northeastern Mediterranean, including Turkey itself, which witnessed political turmoil in early-2013 and borders the already unstable Syria. A crescent of disintegration along the East Mediterranean coastline is indeed a worst-case scenario both for the region itself, and for its NATO partners.[51]

The East Mediterranean and the Arab Spring.

The outbreak of political protest in North Africa and its gradual spread across the Arab world since late-2010, popularly known as the Arab Spring, affected the East Mediterranean as well. Syria has seen a dramatic deterioration of its domestic political situation since early-2011, gradually falling into civil war, which has led to several tens of thousands of human casualties and more than 2.3 million recorded refugees.[52] A series of alleged chemical weapons attacks against Syrian civilians in the suburbs of Damascus in September 2013 led to weeks of debate around a possible international or U.S. military intervention; this debate followed U.S. President Barack Obama's previous declarations that chemical weapons used against civilians in Syria were a "red line" for the United States that would prompt a reconsideration of the U.S. Government's opposition to military intervention.[53] Syria's civil war has led to the cancellation for the time being of all Syrian plans to further explore and develop its offshore Mediterranean oil and gas resources, meaning new discoveries and production capacity from Syria are now expected to be years away, and subject to the stabilization of domestic politics.

Lebanon, into which a large share of Syrian refugees have fled since 2011, appears on the verge of being drawn into the conflict as well, as evident from the resurgence of shooting, assassinations, and sectarian violence. Having been largely spared Arab Spring-related political protests, Lebanon's domestic political life has nevertheless been in deadlock as a result of familiar Lebanese political factors, in addition to the growing threat of resurfacing large-scale sectarian violence.[54] Hence, it comes as little surprise that Lebanese plans to explore and tender out its first offshore blocks have been delayed by more than a year. This was precipitated by the inability of the country's policymaking circles to agree on the sectarian composition of the Petroleum Administration, a body required by the country's petroleum law for the exploration of Lebanese waters to begin.[55] With no government in place throughout most of 2013, further delays are now unavoidable until a new government is able to put into place the decrees required to issue tenders after the country's first bidding round in early-2013.[56]

Lebanon and Syria demonstrate that progress in hydrocarbon development in the East Mediterranean may in reality be halted by domestic politics more than by — as has been widely speculated — cross-border political conflicts. In the case of continued political deadlock in the two countries, prospects for development of East Mediterranean gas resources other than in Cyprus and Israel look unlikely in the near term, promising little positive economic impact other than in those two states. The continuing political destabilization of Lebanon and Syria is highly undesirable, given the impetus of war and political stalemate in a densely populated but heavily compromised region. Instability in Syria and Lebanon also affects regional risk ratings and the attractiveness of foreign investment into regional offshore developments, and thus dilutes any prospect of more comprehensive regional cooperation in both the political and economic spheres.

By contrast, the most recent outbreak of military confrontation in July between the Palestinian organization Hamas and Israel in Gaza has so far had no direct impact on East Mediterranean gas. On the one hand, this is because Palestinian gas is not yet being developed, thereby precluding any impact of the conflict on Palestinian gas; on the other, Israel's gas fields are relatively remote from the conflict point, with Hamas rockets being directed at Israeli land rather than at sea. Once Israeli gas flows into Gaza's now-destroyed sole power plant, theoretically little incentive exists for Palestinian paramilitary groups to bomb their own gas supplies. This contrasts with the already high impact of Egyptian political instability on the likelihood of Israeli gas flowing across the Sinai Peninsula, which is more likely to continue to affect the viability of any onshore pipeline trade option between Israel and Egypt.

NATURAL GAS, REGIONAL COOPERATION, AND THE ROLE OF THE UNITED STATES

The recent East Mediterranean discoveries raise a whole range of commercial and security-related questions: What will the long-term strategy be to monetize the significant value offered by the region's commercial offshore gas and possibly oil resources? Will regional political rivalries, or indeed, domestic political stalemate, hinder the development of these resources over the medium term? Will the East Mediterranean's newly discovered hydrocarbon wealth indeed help the region overcome some of its historical divisions, or will those same divisions be further reinforced by the presence of what looks at present like a significant potential source of new regional income? How will U.S. strategy in the region feed into the direction in which these various factors will play? The possible addition of yet greater offshore hydrocarbon resources — both of natural gas and of oil — alongside the East Mediterranean shores, which also include Syria and Lebanon, will likely add further complexity to the region's already rapidly changing energy security architecture and the direction of future regional energy trade. We examine some of the (currently) most likely regional energy development options, followed by thoughts about the future U.S. role within this newly emerging regional context. It should be noted that the reality is likely to be a combination of different scenarios, as exporter Israel, but potentially also other future East Mediterranean gas producers, will seek security through diversity of export markets.

Scenario 1: Cooperation through regional LNG.

Global trade in LNG has been growing rapidly since the 1990s and, for many new gas producers, has become the method of choice to market their natural gas resources. In the East Mediterranean, too, LNG may capture part of the export volume of natural gas produced, with Cypriot plans to build an LNG liquefaction plant on the southeastern coast of the island, as well as various LNG-related plans currently being discussed by Israel. The outlook of the East Mediterranean as a new LNG-exporting region is hence an interesting prospect.

LNG offers many logistical and—under the right conditions—some commercial advantages over traditional pipeline exports. LNG is flexible and can be exported across regions, eliminating the regional nature of pipeline-dependent natural gas trade and thereby allowing new gas exporters to become players in what is slowly becoming an increasingly global market for natural gas. Global exports, even if (currently) small in total volume, as is the case for the East Mediterranean, hold many geostrategic benefits in addition to the commercial value of reaching new, and potentially premium, markets for gas; it follows that the ability of previously import-dependent countries such as Cyprus, Israel, and Lebanon to supply LNG to Europe, Latin America, or even Asia appears politically attractive both on a domestic and regional level. LNG markets such as Asia-Pacific further promise prospects of substantially higher prices than pipeline gas is likely to fetch in the immediate region or in Europe, despite the need for care over forward-looking price assumptions at a time (2020-30), when pricing structures and price levels are likely to differ significantly from those of today.[57] LNG exports also invite the option for gas producers to engage in the increasingly lucrative spot trade of LNG in addition to long-term contracts, once again adding trade flexibility and potentially raising profits.

The East Mediterranean producers of gas — Cyprus and Israel in particular — also hold very specific reasons to consider LNG over and above pipeline gas. Geographically, Cyprus in particular remains an island state with no overland options for pipeline infrastructure, adding to the cost of pipeline exports via subsea pipelines. The closest subsea route for Cypriot pipeline exports would lead via Turkey, a commercially sensible option but one that is highly unlikely on political grounds (at the time of this writing), given the continually unresolved Cyprus question and Turkey's consequent reluctance to trade with the Republic of Cyprus.[58] An alternative pipeline route to Greece, while politically more desirable, involves a significant geographical diversion of a Cypriot pipeline route, more than tripling the distance to land, while the eventual market price paid by Greece — like Cyprus still at the verge of financial collapse — is unlikely to be anywhere near enough to justify the enormous additional cost of a subsea pipeline connecting the two remotest parts of Europe. Other pipeline routes could connect Cyprus via subsea pipelines to Israel or Egypt — both natural gas producers in their own right — but both displaying a high degree of significant political problems that are unlikely to render them desirable transit locations for Cypriot gas in the first place.

Israel itself, being a political more than a geographical island inside the Levant, faces a history of complicated political relations with its Arab neighbors; it has been at war with all of them at different points of time since its establishment in 1948. Given the continued de facto war with neighbors Syria and Lebanon, any gas trade with Israel's northern neighbors is unlikely in the near future; nor is it possible for Israel to export natural gas via existing pipeline infrastructure onward to Turkey using the land route via Lebanon and/or Syria. Relations with southern neighbors Jordan and Egypt and the Palestinians have, by contrast, been more varied and would, in principle, allow for pipeline trade. However, those elements inside Israel who would oppose natural gas trade with Arab neighbors on political grounds, in addition to uncertainty over the viability of these trade routes, render LNG for Israel, as much as for Cyprus, a regionally independent gas-export option with significant commercial potential under the right circumstances.[59]

Individual LNG or a Regional LNG Hub?

Cyprus has already embraced LNG exports as its main export strategy for the early-2020s — not least because of significant interest by operating companies Noble and its partners in monetizing Cypriot gas in the most commercially straightforward way.[60] Disappointing appraisal drilling results in October 2013 have for the time being cast doubts over the commercial viability of an LNG terminal in Cyprus as long as no additional resources are found offshore Cyprus or brought in from neighboring countries sharing a potential LNG terminal, such as Israel. Potential cooperation between Cyprus and Israel over shared LNG facilities at Vassilikos has been discussed in the media and by political and commercial interest groups. A regional LNG hub on Cyprus would solve two parallel problems. Cyprus could attract additional funding and investment, making use of economies of scale, while raising the commercial viability of LNG exports under the current time plan in case of less-than-expected eventual production rates for Block 12, the only block currently far enough explored to start production by producer Noble's ambitious time schedule. This argument has gained additional urgency following Noble's sobering results from its second appraisal drilling in October 2013, which some observers have interpreted as throwing back Cypriot LNG export plans by up to 2 years if no additional gas can be sourced.[61]

Israel, on the other hand, would similarly benefit in financial terms from the arrangement, saving investment costs for a new greenfield project inside Israeli territory, while solving the politically controversial question of where to place an Israeli LNG export terminal along the country's crowded and terror-prone coastline. Similar factors affect Lebanon's gas export plans, since if Lebanon's own potential offshore gas production materializes in the coming years, Lebanon too could be a potential partner for a Cyprus-based regional LNG hub. Lebanese and Israeli cooperation with Cyprus over LNG exports will obviously be mutually exclusive — implying a head start for Israel, whose gas development program is significantly more advanced than that of Lebanon — while a potential Israeli alteration of plans to reserve its gas production for domestic supply or regional pipeline trade could open a window of opportunity for Lebanon at a later stage.

Opponents to an Israeli-Cypriot entente, primarily within Israel, fear Israeli dependence on a third country for Israeli gas exports, which may expose Israel to the use of its gas export facilities as political leverage, in addition to reduced tax revenues for the Israeli state.[62] Shared Cypriot-Israeli LNG facilities also hold the potential for diplomatic interference with Israel's parallel strategy of improving political and commercial relations with neighboring Turkey, with discussions over Israeli pipeline exports to Turkey ongoing in parallel to talks with Cyprus. In the case of exacerbation of armed conflict within Cyprus, Israeli gas exports, moreover, might be held hostage alongside Cypriot gas, a prospect that will cause unease in Israeli policy circles despite its relative unlikelihood at present.

The expected volume of East Mediterranean LNG exports under a best-case scenario throughout the 2020s should be seen as moderate in size. Cyprus's initial plans were for initially one LNG train of around 5-10 million metric tons per annum in the early-2020s, possibly to be added to in subsequent years by one or two more trains, although current reserve corrections seem to disallow this target. Israel, if and when it decides to export LNG, may add an additional one to two trains. Even in the currently unclear case of another, possibly Lebanese, LNG train to come on stream by the late-2020s, this volume is no strategic competitor to the new, large LNG exporters, Australia, East Africa, and, possibly, the United States, over key premium markets in Asia.[63] Hence, the overwhelming commercial success of Cypriot LNG is by no means guaranteed, despite obvious economic potential in principle. Floating LNG (FLNG), too, could be an option, in particular as it would offer an answer to smaller 3-5-tcf fields such as Block 12 and Tamar, in addition to its application on larger fields such as Leviathan. The technology for this would need to be brought in by an outside company, since experience in

FLNG, a relatively new technology option,[64] remains limited to a handful of international companies. While Woodside, for instance, has been strongly advocating FLNG in Israel, the question is which company would supply the technology, given the possible negative implications for any company with Arab country exposure. Cyprus may find it easier to attract a range of experienced companies, but the Cypriot government's past focus on onshore LNG renders this option, so far, one with no systematic policy focus in Cyprus.

Scenario 2: Regional Pipeline Trade.

Looking beyond LNG, there are many important reasons to consider the potential role East Mediterranean gas could play in regional exports. The Middle East and North Africa are among the world's fastest-growing regional demand centers for natural gas, and despite significant gas reserves there is an increasing shortfall of gas production to satisfy domestic market demand. Energy Information Agency (EIA) projections suggest total Middle Eastern gas demand will almost double until 2040, rendering the Middle East second only to Asia-Pacific in the rate of its market growth for several decades to come (see Figures 1 and 2). Turkey, another rapidly growing energy market bordering the East Mediterranean, is also a potential market for East Mediterranean gas, as well, because of its strategic geographical location. Turkey is an important future transit hub for pipeline gas from West and Central Asia to Europe, as part of European efforts to diversify their gas supplies away from Russia via the Southern Corridor.[65]

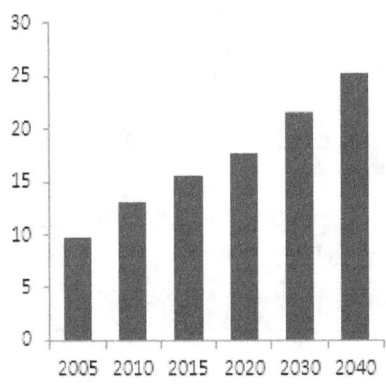

Note: The Middle East includes Bahrain, Iran, Iraq, Israel, Jordan, Kuwait, Lebanon, Oman, Qatar, Saudi Arabia, Syria, the United Arab Emirates (UAE), and Yemen.

Source: EIA, Washington, DC, 2014.

Figure 1. Projected Natural Gas Demand in the Middle East (bcf), 2010-40.

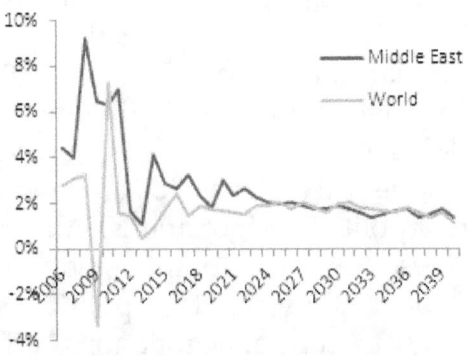

Note: The Middle East includes Bahrain, Iran, Iraq, Israel, Jordan, Kuwait, Lebanon, Oman, Qatar, Saudi Arabia, Syria, the UAE, and Yemen.

Source: EIA (2014)

Figure 2. Projected Natural Gas Demand Growth in the Middle East (Percentage), 2010-40.

An Arab-Israeli "Peace Pipeline"?

Part of Israel's options to market and monetize its natural gas lie in its direct regional neighborhood, and a series of initial agreements with Israel's Arab neighbors since early-2014 indicates that Israel is indeed positively inclined toward these options. The Palestinian Territories, economically marginalized and with no energy resources beyond the so-far-undeveloped offshore Gaza Marine, proved indeed to be the first Israeli gas customers in January 2014. After several months of private negotiations, Palestine Power Generation Co. signed an agreement to purchase around 4.75-bcm of natural gas over a 20-year period, worth some \$1.2 bn,[66] an initial agreement followed in subsequent months by similar agreements with Union Fenosa and BG Group in Egypt over the potential supply of some 1.75-tcf of Israeli gas to Egyptian markets, and up to 3.75-tcf for export as LNG through Egypt's since late-2013 largely idle liquefaction plants.[67] The Israeli-Palestinian entente came amidst reintensified efforts by international and U.S. diplomats to forge a greater Middle East peace agreement, contrasting with years of unsuccessful attempts to gain tangible results from broader political negotiations. An *International Business Times* commentator pointedly contrasted the decades of fruitless effort on political settlement with what a few months of negotiations between commercial companies on both sides have been able to achieve.[68]

While the volume of gas and the value of the trade agreement are not large by the standards of potential Israeli or Cypriot gas exports via LNG into international markets, or even by pipeline into larger regional energy markets, the Israeli-Palestinian gas trade agreement symbolizes the political and commercial viability of regional pipeline exports, including from Israel. While politically appealing from an Israeli perspective (Palestinian dependence on Israeli gas for the security of electricity supplied to Palestinian homes ideally reduces the incentives for Palestinian politicians to forge a new full-scale military conflict with Israel), the trade deal is also economically beneficial for both sides. On the one hand, Israel earns export revenues involving only a small volume of Israeli gas (in contrast with the high-volume, long-term contracts associated, for instance, with LNG exports that are opposed in Israel on political grounds). The Palestinian Authority and Palestine Power pay significantly less for Israeli gas than they would for the alternative of high-cost international oil imports, which, so far, are the only fuel alternative to natural gas for the Palestinians in view of the lack of gas supplies anywhere in their regional vicinity.[69]

This mutually beneficial trade arrangement between Israelis and Palestinians could also be extendable into Israel's other Arab neighborhoods; both Jordan and Egypt are growing gas markets, short of natural gas supplies — in the case of Egypt, this is also due to lacking domestic investment, exacerbated by more than 3 years of political turmoil following the Arab Spring — and economically overburdened by existing government spending. Alternative fuel imports from international markets are high-cost options, with costs for oil imports having more than doubled over the 2000s as a result of rising oil prices and Jordan and Egypt's continuingly high reliance on oil-fired power generation.[70] Jordan signed a gas trading agreement with Israel in February 2014 worth $500 million, with the option to turn Israel into Jordan's main supplier over the coming years.[71] Commercially speaking, this gas trading agreement is likely to be the lowest-cost energy supply option available to Jordan over the coming years—a truth likely applicable to Egypt as well.

While Jordan relies on international loans, Egypt currently survives on financial and in-kind aid from several Gulf Cooperation Council countries, primarily Saudi Arabia, Qatar, the UAE, and Kuwait.[72] For Egypt, too, any medium- to long-term energy supply option will rest on a low-cost fuel supply, with Israel ironically offering the most likely competitively priced gas option. In addition to the cost of fuel, the largely pre-existing pipeline infrastructure connecting the three countries—because of Egypt's historical gas exports to both Israel and Jordan—implies that capital costs for an initial infrastructure investment would be low and, unlike in the case of Israeli LNG, would not require 20-year contracts to finance the entire initial capital cost.[73] (See Figures 3 and 4.)

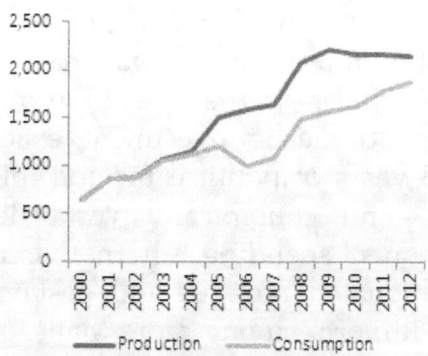

Source: EIA, Washington, DC, 2014.

Figure 3. Egypt's Narrowing Domestic Gas Balance (bcf per annum).

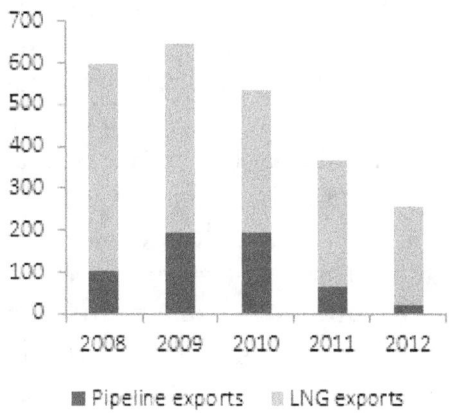

Source: EIA, Washington, DC, 2013, with data from BP and Cedigaz.

Figure 4. Egypt's Pipeline and LNG Exports (bcf/a).

Both Jordan and Egypt also offer additional benefits to the Israeli side, which, in turn, may positively influence the price of Israeli gas supplied to these markets. Egypt already has two LNG liquefaction plants, both of which operate below capacity because of Egypt's domestic gas shortage, with long-term supply contracts in principle tying Egyptian gas into export markets.[74] Israeli gas could supply these LNG facilities, using existing infrastructure rather than constructing new facilities in the East Mediterranean, and capturing the LNG market share—possibly via gas swaps with Egypt—thereby solving both Egypt's problem of fulfilling supply contract conditions, while offering Israel access to LNG markets. Similarly, Jordan has been considering turning its Red Sea port of Aqaba into an LNG hub, and could host a yet to-be-built LNG facility that could export Israeli, or possibly later, Lebanese

LNG, with an eye on premium Asian markets.[75] In this context, Jordan may prove to be an even more attractive option than Egypt, given that Suez Canal fees can be avoided while reaching Asian markets. Both Jordan and Egypt could benefit from the resultant transit fees, while the mutually beneficial trade arrangement between them and Israel would likely forge beneficial political stability across gas-transiting borders; Jordan would also see additional infrastructure investment, providing a new technology branch, foreign investment and new employment options. The resulting pipeline trade scenario would resemble only at first sight a regional "peace pipeline" approach; in reality, it could be a fully functioning and commercially very beneficial arrangement for both the Arab and the Israeli sides.

The most important stumbling block to such a regional solution will undoubtedly be politics, on both sides. Israeli politicians, some of whom remain opposed to any Israeli gas exports, have dominated public debates and tried to block the Israeli government's decision to allow gas exports rather than reserve Israel's newly found hydrocarbon wealth for the domestic market. On the Jordanian-Egyptian sides, many political groups and a majority of the population will be opposed to natural gas trade on political grounds. The Palestinian cause, including continuingly unresolved questions such as Palestinian statehood and land claims, Jewish settlements, and the status of Jerusalem and of several million Palestinian refugees (1.9 million of which have been registered by the United Nations in Jordan alone)[76] resonates with a vast part of these countries' populations and renders the idea of Jordanian and Egyptian gas payments contributing to Israel's security budget deeply uncomfortable.

Egypt's natural gas trade deal under the Mubarak regime during the 2000s sparked political protest and heated debate, with some civil society institutions taking the administration to court to stop Egyptian gas exports to Israel.[77] Moreover, Jordan's King Abdallah II and the ruling Hashemite family rely on political support from East Bank tribal families, the loss of whose support over a Jordanian-Israeli gas trade deal would come at an unacceptable political cost.[78] Also, trade with Israel in natural gas would render its Arab trade partners—Jordan and Egypt, to very different extents—dependent on Israeli gas deliveries, providing Israel with a powerful strategic ransom in the case of any new outbreak of military confrontation.

REGIONAL PIPELINE GAS INTO TURKEY AND EUROPE

Turkey is another potentially significant export partner for Israel, and, in the much-longer term, once the Cypriot question is resolved, an export partner for Cyprus. Turkey is a rapidly growing demand market, the largest in the wider region, with some of the highest regional domestic gas prices. This also renders the Turkish market attractive for supply projects involving an initially higher capital cost, such as for long-distance and subsea pipelines. For Cyprus itself, a direct subsea pipeline to Turkey would entail the lowest capital costs of any export option, although politics are unlikely to render this option palatable at the time of this writing. Even from Israel, a subsea pipeline link to Turkey has been assessed as logistically and commercially feasible, and would be for Israel the only option to reach Turkey by pipeline while the land route via Lebanon and Syria remains closed. (See Figure 5.)

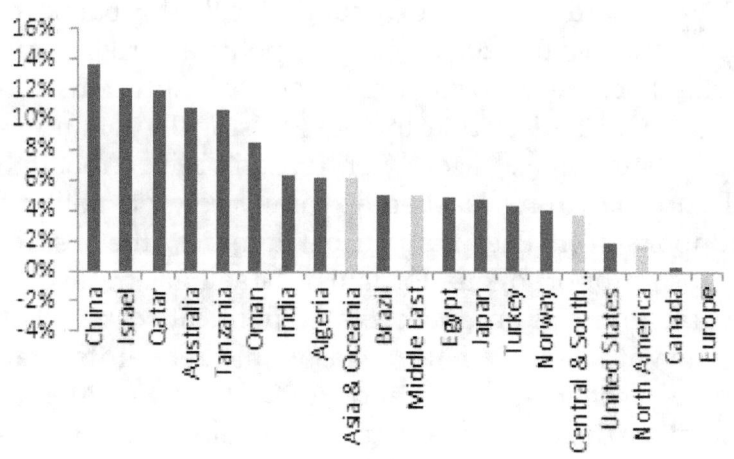

Source: Authors, based on EIA, Washington, DC, 2013.

**Figure 5. Natural Gas Consumption,
5-yr Compound Average Annual Growth, 2008-12,
Selected Countries and Regions.**

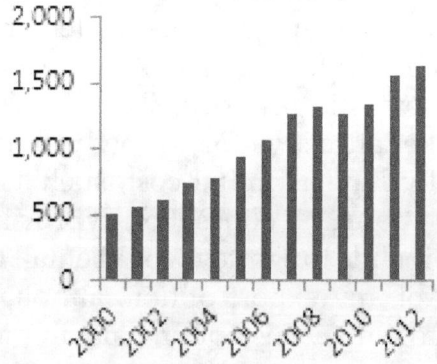

Source: EIA, Washington, DC, 2013.

Figure 6. Turkey's Growing Gas Market, bcf.

Strategically, Turkey offers further attractions. Turkish interests in promoting itself as a new gas transit hub for European gas would also offer East Mediterranean gas exporters the long-term prospect of 1 day exporting gas to Europe, albeit in small volumes.[79] The commercial value of East Mediterranean gas exports to Europe may be moderate, and would still entail more questions from the producers' sides regarding the price Europe is likely to pay for new gas contracts in view of the changing European gas pricing environment. However, the strategic value of East Mediterranean gas exports into Europe may be high, given European interests in diversifying sources of the gas supply away from traditional Russian supplies are also important political considerations. The 2014 Ukraine crisis, which (at the time of this writing) has led to the imposition of U.S. and European sanctions against Russia in the aftermath of the alleged shooting down of Malaysia Airlines flight MH17 in July 2014 over Ukrainian territory, has arguably added further strategic value to any future alternative gas supply for Southeastern Europe. Cypriot gas sold to Turkey, and potentially onward to Europe, could also constitute an important basis for renewed peace talks between the two sides, providing an important commercial carrot for the pursuit of specific outcomes of any negotiations between the two sides. Similarly, Israeli gas sold to Turkey via the Cypriot exclusive economic zone could benefit Cyprus by way of parallel gas supply and transit fees. It could also open the Turkish route, albeit initially only for Israeli gas, on the Cypriot side, while providing Turkey with a gas corridor that could be further opened up to Cypriot gas in the future if political tensions ease.[80]

Israeli-Turkish relations have undergone various phases, having been troubled by ideological differences as well as the 2010 killing of Turkish Palestine activists on a Turkish ship off Israel's coasts. Both Turkey and Israel could nevertheless have considerable interest in gas trade, because of the commercial attractiveness of the option. Turkey also has an intrinsic interest in gas supply options other than dominant supplier Russia, while its main alternative, Iran, has been under sanctions and appears an unlikely incremental supplier for Turkey's fast-rising gas demand.[81] Other supply options for Turkey are complicated, for apart from the cost-intensive option of LNG, other regional supplies from Iraq and the Caspian — politically charged in their own right — have not been forthcoming. Former U.S. Ambassador Matt Bryza sees a possible advantageous entente:

> A pipeline connecting Leviathan to the Turkish market, the most commercially efficient export option, could help resurrect a strategic partnership dedicated to regional prosperity and stability between Israel and Turkey.[82]

The Israeli-Turkish option, because of its comparably lesser political hurdle, is also the most probable medium-term option for East Mediterranean gas exports into Turkey. Besides political will on both sides, one of the key obstacles to overcome in order to enable both countries to trade with each other is undoubtedly a solution to the two countries' conflict over the Gaza flotilla incident, at which nine political activists supporting the political cause of the Palestinians in Gaza — including eight Turkish citizens — were killed by Israeli soldiers during a military raid.[83] After the Turkish downgrading of relations to second secretary level and cooling bilateral relations thereafter, a telephone conversation in March 2013 between Turkish Prime Minister Recep Tayyip Erdogan and Israeli Prime Minister Benjamin Netanyahu—during which Netanyahu apologized for operational mistakes by Israel during the flotilla incident—has since raised hopes for a rapprochement of the two sides.[84] A likely next step will involve financial compensation for the families of those killed in the incident, after which gas trade relations between Israel and Turkey may well be a politically palatable option. The role of international intermediaries such as the United States could well consist of political support for this reconciliation process, providing forums and overall policy support where required.

The Cypriot-Turkish case is significantly more complicated, and looks difficult in the absence of a more comprehensive peace arrangement and the distribution of resource revenues from the export of Cypriot gas exports among all Cypriot citizens, including in the North. International intermediation and diplomatic efforts once more provide an essential background to progress in the matter. So does American mediation and policy support alongside the EU in facilitating talks and trust-building mechanisms that would render Cypriot-Turkish gas trade a desirable long-term outcome of fruitful negotiation.

U.S. Diplomatic and Security Cooperation.

U.S. diplomatic and military support has a pivotal role to play in the East Mediterranean's complex geopolitical landscape, and its importance will only grow as the value of the natural resources at stake increases. On the Western part of the East Mediterranean, both

Cyprus and Turkey are important partners for U.S. interests in different regions. Cyprus is a NATO partner and a long-term strategic ally of Europe and the United States in the East Mediterranean. It is wedged between Europe, Eurasia, and the Middle East and, as such, is a perfect location for regionally based intelligence and defense systems. Turkey is a NATO partner and a key location for the stationing of a U.S. early-warning-radar system as part of the NATO missile defense system for Europe. It is an important U.S. ally with an interest in regional democratic transition and stability, and is a political buffer between Europe on the one hand, and unstable neighboring countries Syria, Iraq, and Iran on the other.[85] Making regional gas developments and trade an economic pillar in U.S. foreign engagement in the region could be a highly beneficial way of concentrating resources in a region that may yet listen to economic incentives after many decades of unsuccessful, politically motivated rounds of negotiation.

Diplomatically, the U.S. role could entail a whole range of areas for mediation, and for contributing to the realization of different East Mediterranean project options. Within the Cypriot-Turkish knot, as well as on the side of Israeli-Turkish relations, ample scope exists for the intensification of diplomatic efforts that would help Cyprus develop its offshore resources peacefully and without ensuing conflict with mainland Turkey. In this context, the current diplomatic crisis between Russia, the EU, and the United States could serve as an important basis for future efforts by American and European partners to foster diplomatic talks between the two Cypriot communities on the one hand, and Turkey on the other, to create an environment more conductive to the export of East Mediterranean gas to

Europe through the Turkish route. Furthermore, and in the case of LNG, a Cypriot LNG terminal as currently planned does not require a benevolent Turkish stance toward Cypriot exports, nor a comprehensive peace agreement between the Cypriot communities. Nevertheless, stable relationships would help remove barriers that could later on threaten Vassilikos LNG, such as the Turkish-Cypriot contestation of Cypriot exploration and production efforts, and the possible exacerbation of maritime border disagreements into armed violence. The ideal inroads to prevent such scenarios would likely involve:

1. A rapprochement between the Greek- and Turkish-Cypriot communities, supporting LNG export plans from Vassilikos and the secure development of hydrocarbon resources from tendered-out exploration blocks;

2. A Turkish-Cypriot rapprochement that enables the above; and,

3. A Turkish-Israeli détente that helps the two countries overcome mutual animosities.

International efforts to promote a comprehensive settlement of the Cypriot question have been ongoing for many decades. Natural gas discoveries could facilitate the process. However, the vital interests of both European and U.S. partners of Cyprus in the resolution of the issue render continuous, intensified efforts in this direction ever more important. Cyprus's natural gas development offers a powerful carrot for new and intensified regional talks and the introduction of a new regional roadmap to peace and cooperation over these new natural resources. The United States, as an intermediary, is of prime importance in this regard. A diplomatic ally both of Europe and of the Republic of

Cyprus, it is also a NATO partner of Turkey, thereby enjoying mutual respect and relations with both political sides. Meanwhile, American diplomatic strength could prove critical in engaging all sides constructively in both open- and closed-door meetings.

On the Middle Eastern side, any escalation of territorial disputes over offshore hydrocarbon resources between Israel and Lebanon in particular would call for U.S. support, and before that, diplomatic efforts to reduce the risk of any outbreak of conflict. U.S.-Israeli economic, diplomatic, and defense ties have been close for many decades.[86] It was partly as a result of U.S. diplomatic efforts that Israel and the Palestinian Liberation Organization returned to the negotiation table for direct talks over a comprehensive peace agreement, an effort that has brought the United States much recognition throughout the Arab world. The agreement between Israelis and Palestinians to trade in natural gas has been one detail within these negotiations. However, this agreement underlines the considerable potential that well-directed U.S. diplomatic efforts can achieve, particularly after several years of stalled relations among all three sides. There are numerous precedents for the joint exploration and exploitation of disputed territories for natural resources, which could be considered for similar cases in the East Mediterranean, once more raising the potential benefits of U.S. intermediation.[87]

U.S. interests also involve the peaceful exploitation of the Levant's hydrocarbon wealth for reasons beyond Israel's sake; both neighboring Syria and Lebanon remain key players on the region's geopolitical map, underlying U.S. political calculations vis-à-vis neighboring Iran.[88] Economic and political chaos in the two states, possibly fueled further by escalating conflict with Israel, or between Lebanon and Syria over their own respective maritime boundaries, might contribute to a strengthening of those regional political influences that U.S. policymakers would undoubtedly prefer to avoid. Neither does Israel benefit from unstable neighboring states, for the potential for growth in politically radical elements, in support of or parallel to existing political groups such as Hezbollah, poses additional security risks to Israel's own territory. Jordan and Egypt, on the other hand, are recipients of substantial amounts of U.S. foreign aid, rendering economic solutions to their long-standing domestic energy woes, such as low-cost Israeli gas, a potential area of interest for U.S. diplomatic efforts for reasons beyond the clear political and economic policy considerations that will likely exist in Israeli policy circles.[89] Both countries have struck historical peace deals with Israel, and Jordan's role in the Middle East Peace Process, in the Syrian Civil War (by taking in Syrian refugees), and U.S.-Jordanian military and intelligence cooperation[90] render a facilitating U.S. role in Israeli-Jordanian talks over mutual gas trade a potential area for U.S. involvement.

U.S. diplomatic efforts have also been, and should continue to be, directed at finding a comprehensive peace agreement between Israelis and Palestinians that ends the decades-long stalemate that has led to deeply unsatisfying outcomes for both sides. Israeli as well as Palestinian offshore hydrocarbon resources could play a significant role in facilitating mutual trust and the willingness to cooperate, including between Israel and a few of its other Arab neighbors, Jordan and Egypt. Palestinian gas offshore Gaza furthermore provides a potentially valuable economic prize, the development of which could be tied to the stabilization of Israeli-Palestinian ties and the rebuilding of the now wartorn Gaza Strip and the Palestinian economy as a whole. It is, nevertheless, important to realize the limitations of the approach of "peace pipelines" to cement peace where underlying political disagreements remain unresolved. Therefore, using gas for the purpose of solving political problems that remain unrelated to gas is a trap that should be carefully avoided. U.S. diplomatic support may also be specifically needed in the already existing conflict between Israel and Lebanon about the disputed maritime territory across the 2,000 blue line — with ongoing U.S. mediation between the two parties to the conflict being an important contribution to reducing the possibility of escalation into military conflict.[91]

In the event of escalating regional tensions, the United States also holds an important military position that could have an impact in securing the East Mediterranean. Prospects for regional LNG exports, based on Cyprus, with the possibility of Israeli and later Lebanese LNG exports, raise the potential for essential gas infrastructure to become a target of politically motivated sabotage, terrorist attacks, and, in the case of cross-border military conflict, military attacks against LNG infrastructure on a much greater scale than is currently possible. LNG plants, while in principle not as dangerous a target as already traveling oil transport freighters in the East Mediterranean, offer a highly symbolic target for attack, and unlike the subsea pipeline infrastructure, are just as visible as oil platforms. The additional potential for liquids production from several East Mediterranean wells further adds to the explosive potential that any targeted attack against natural gas production platforms in the Mediterranean Sea could have. Limited distances between East Mediterranean neighbors means that in many cases, results such as the destruction of gas and oil production platforms and subsequent oil spills into the East Mediterranean Sea would likely affect neighboring countries as well; the densely populated coastlines of Gaza, Israel, and Lebanon mean substantial parts of the populations could suffer collateral damage from attacks against land infrastructure such as onshore LNG export facilities and gas production plants.

In Israel in particular, the prospect of an onshore LNG plant along the crowded Israeli coastline and its potential to become the target of terrorist attacks has fueled a domestic debate about the desirability of LNG exports via an Israeli land facility in the first place—adding to those advocates calling for the total cancellation of Israeli gas export plans for reasons of energy security. Even in the case of offshore FLNG export facilities or a shared LNG facility on Vassilikos, Israeli LNG plants could still be the targets of terrorist activity or military attacks in case of an armed cross-border conflict after all; indeed, the potential for Cyprus to be drawn into such a conflict through attacks against joint Israeli-Cypriot facilities will need to be considered. U.S. military training and equipment support, and a U.S. diplomatic position supportive of both Cyprus and Israel in case of any third party's attack against their energy infrastructure and gas developments, could prove essential in this equation.

CONCLUSION AND FINAL RECOMMENDATIONS

The East Mediterranean region, with its multiplicity of long-standing, unresolved political and territorial disputes and conflicts—a jigsaw of different political and economic interests geographically located where Europe, Eurasia, and the Middle East intercept—remains of critical geostrategic importance for U.S. interests. The recent discoveries of sizeable hydrocarbon resources, placed in the region's former context of energy-import dependency, provides a significant opportunity to strengthen regional cooperation in a way that benefits all sides but also holds much potential to complicate further the region's conflict-prone geopolitical architecture. U.S. support, driven by key U.S. interests in the area, eventually may prove critical to help shape the way in which natural resources define the East Mediterranean's regional security landscape over the coming years. In particular:

- The stability of Cyprus is of great importance to the continuity of U.S. military and intelligence operations. To retain U.S. military communications facilities on the island, the U.S. Government should continue its efforts to support the improvement of Cypriot-Turkish relations and to ensure that conflicting interests and overlapping claims do not deteriorate to the point of a conflict between two of its NATO allies.
- Israel's security, and the stability of the Levant—in particular the Israel-Lebanon, Israel-Jordan, and Israel-Palestinian Territories borders—lies at the heart of U.S. foreign policy in the region. U.S. mediation to help find a sustainable *modus operandi* for the disputed territories, such as joint exploration and production or the sharing of revenues could help prevent further escalation into military conflict, with the potential to destabilize the already fragile region further.

- U.S. security and military support for its main allies in the case of an eruption of natural resource conflict in the East Mediterranean may prove essential in managing possible future conflict; this involves cooperation in areas such as intelligence and nonlethal security as well as the evaluation of different risks associated with the region's various export options.

U.S. experience in information operations and strategic communications can help its partners in the East Mediterranean craft their strategy for creating public support for any negotiated regional gas trading and cooperation framework. The lack of supportive public sentiment in Egypt for collaborating with Israel, for instance, is one of the key challenges to initiating any commercial negotiations. The sustainable success of a cooperation agreement depends on a capability to study systematically and understand different audiences in a specific context to inform policy and shape impactful communications messages. It should also be obvious that any absence of visible U.S. diplomatic and technical assistance could lead to a gradual change of alliances among some parts of the region toward emerging powers and potential new peace brokers such as Russia — which already entertains a strong interest in East Mediterranean gas developments — and notably China.

Finally, the East Mediterranean hydrocarbon discoveries offer the region's economies a very real chance to transform their domestic economies and their energy mixes, thereby creating viable long-term growth and economic prosperity. U.S. support — diplomatic and, where necessary, military — can form a potentially powerful element in the safeguarding of these long-term economic benefits, at little cost in relative terms. In the wake of the political unrest and frustration that has swept the Arab streets since early-2010, and Cyprus's continuing difficult financial position, this would be no small success. It would be no less so in view of the added benefit of political peace and stability in one of the world's most conflicted regional security systems in the 20th and 21st century.

ENDNOTES

1. "East Mediterranean Region," *Country Analysis Brief*, Washington, DC: U.S. Energy Information Administration (EIA), August 15, 2013, available from *www.eia.gov/countries/regions-topics. cfm?fips=EM*.

2. A full profile of Syria as an oil and gas producer can be found at *Syria Country Analysis Brief*, Washington, DC: EIA, February 18, 2014, available from *www.eia.gov/countries/cab.cfm?fips=SY*.

3. Hakim Darbouche, Laura El-Katiri, and Bassam Fattouh, "East Mediterranean Gas: What Kind of Game Changer?" *Research Paper*, Oxford, UK: Oxford Institute for Energy Studies, December 2012, available from *www.oxfordenergy.org/wpcms/wp-content/ uploads/2012/12/NG-71.pdf*; Energy balance data for all East Mediterranean countries can be found at EIA International Energy Statistics database, 2014, available from *www.eia.gov/cfapps/ipdb project/IEDIndex3.cfm*.

4. Brenda Schaffer, "Israel—New Natural Gas Producer in the Mediterranean," *Energy Policy*, Vol. 39, 2011, p. 5,379; see also Simon Henderson, "Energy Discoveries in the Eastern Mediterranean: Source for Cooperation or Fuel for Tension? The Case of Israel," *GMF Policy Brief*, Washington, DC: The German Marshall Fund of the United States, June 2012.

5. Darbouche, El-Katiri, and Fattouh, p. 9.

6. "Overview of Oil and Natural Gas in the Eastern Mediterranean Region," *Analysis Brief*, Washington, DC: EIA, Au-

gust 15, 2013, available from *www.eia.gov/countries/regions-topics. cfm?fips=EM*; see also Schaffer.

7. Walid Khadduri, "The East Mediterranean Offshore Petroleum Frontier," *Middle East Economic Survey*, Vol. 53, Issue 44, November 1, 2010.

8. Schaffer; Shoshanna Solomon, and Gwen Ackerman, "Israel Starts Tamar Gas Production," *Bloomberg*, May 31, 2013.

9. "Noble Energy Announces Significant Discovery at Leviathan Offshore Israel," *Offshore Energy Today*, December 30, 2010; Amiram Barkat, "Noble CEO: Leviathan Is Largest Gas Find in Our History, "' *The Jerusalem Post*, December 29, 2010.

10. Schaffer; Khadduri.

11. Proven reserves from International Energy Statistics 2013, Washington, DC: EIA; Total estimate by authors.

12. Anastasios Giamouridis, "The Offshore Discovery in the Republic of Cyprus Monetisation Prospects and Challenges," OIES Research Paper, NG 65, Oxford, UK: Oxford Institute for Energy Studies, July 2012; see also Anastasios Giamouridis, "Natural Gas in Cyprus. Choosing the Right Option," GMF Mediterranean Paper Series, Washington DC: The German Marshall Fund of the United States, September 23, 2013.

13. "Noble Estimates Cyprus Reserves at 3-9 Tcf, Eyes Israeli LNG Export," *Natural Gas Week*, November 21, 2011. A previous independent estimate by consultants Netherland Sewell and Associates (NSAI) in early-March 2011 put Aphrodite's mean reserves at 5.1-tcf, with a 50-percent probability. Noble, which works with a gross mean estimate of 7-tcf, dismissed these estimates, stating that NSAI utilized a "deterministic" calculation of resources, the results of which were "not directly comparable to the 'probabilistic' calculation." See, MEES, Vol. 55, Issue 12, March 19, 2012, pp. 5-8.

14. "Total Signs on Deepwater Blocks Southwest of Cyprus," *Oil and Gas Journal*, February 6, 2013; "ENI/Kogas Secure Deal For Cyprus Offshore Gas Exploration," *Middle East Economic Survey*, February 4, 2013.

15. *"Syria Country Analysis Brief,"* Washington, DC: EIA, February 18, 2014, available from *www.eia.gov/countries/cab. cfm?fips=SY*. At the time of this writing, Syria's oil exports to Turkey and Europe are disrupted.

16. Syrian officials at the time blamed this on high exploration costs and low oil prices, but the reality includes probably poor seismic data and high resultant investment risk, coupled with expectedly unattractive rates of returns for international investors.

17. Laura El-Katiri, Bassam Fattouh, and Richard Mallinson, "The Arab Uprisings and MENA Political Instability: Implications for Oil and Gas markets," OIES Paper: MEP 8, Oxford, UK: Oxford Institute for Energy Studies, March 2014, available from *www.oxfordenergy.org/wpcms/wp-content/uploads/2014/03/ME P-8.pdf*.

18. An overview of European sanctions is provided by the UK government, available from *www.gov.uk/government/ publications/financial-sanctions-syria*.

19. For example, see "Formation of Lebanon Panel Paves Way for Bid Round," *International Oil Daily*, November 12, 2012. For a comprehensive analysis of Lebanon's prospects as a future gas producer, see B. Fattouh and L. El-Katiri, "Lebanon: the Next East Mediterranean Gas Producer?" Mediterranean Paper Series, Washington, DC: The German Marshall Fund of the United States, forthcoming 2015.

20. "Political Stalemate Scaring Off Oil Bidders," *The Daily Star*, August 15, 2013; Lubnan ja'lanu, "an ihtiati ghaz dhakhm bimiahihi" ("Lebanon Announces Large Natural Gas Reserves in its Waters"), *Al Jazeera*, September 24, 2013; "Al-wazir: taqdirat tushiru liwujud ghaz wan aft bi-kamiyyat kabira fi ma lubnan" ("Minister: Estimates Indicate the Existence of Oil and Gas in Large Quantities in Lebanon"), *Reuters Arabic*, October 27, 2013.

21. "Bassil: Lebanon Has 30 Trillion Cubic Feet of Gas, 660 Million Oil Barrels," *Naharnet Newsdesk*, May 10, 2013.

22. Schaffer, 2011.

23. Avi Bar-Eli, "Ya'alon: British Gas Natural Gas Deal in Gaza Will Finance Terror," *Haaretz*, October 21, 2007, available from *www.haaretz.com/news/ya-alon-british-gas-natural-gas-deal-in-gaza-will-finance-terror-1.231576*; "BG Said to Sell Gas Field Off Gaza after Israel Blocks Project," *Bloomberg*, March 9, 2012.

24. A look at some of the world's major disputes over territory and natural resources illustrates the size of the problem, for instance, the ongoing dispute between North and South Sudan over the oil-rich region of Abyei, and continued conflict between Iraq's central government and the Kurdish regional government over ownership of local hydrocarbon resources. For instance, see "Sudan and South Sudan," Washington, DC: EIA, September 5, 2013, available from *www.eia.gov/countries/analysisbriefs/Sudan/sudan.pdf*.

25. Paul Rivlin, "The Significance of Gas in the East Mediterranean," *Iqtisadi*, Vol. 3, No. 9, October 16, 2013.

26. *Ibid.*

27. Previous studies of the Palestinian gas market suggested that Gaza Marine, the main field discovered offshore the coast of Gaza, would be comparatively easy to develop, given its proximity to the coastline and low depth. It would easily feed the Palestinian market's limited domestic demand of around 0.3-bcm per year during the early-2010s, and could thus allow up to 1-bcm/yr of additional gas to be exported to neighboring markets, for instance, Egypt, Jordan, or—relevant during the early-2000s when Israel was looking for import supplies—Israel. Gas for the Palestinian market could be used in the existing 140-MW Gaza power plant, as well as two planned gas-fired power stations in the West Bank, contributing both to secure electricity supplies and a source of revenue for the stagnating Palestinian economy. For instance, see "No Advance Towards Development for Offshore Gaza Marine," *Middle East Economic Survey*, Issue 55, Vol. 40, September 28, 2012.

28. For a background, see *Ibid.*; Walid Khadduri, "Gaza Gas: Challenges Versus Opportunities," *Oxford Energy Forum*, August 2013, pp. 28-30; David Wurmser, "The Geopolitics of Israel's Offshore Gas Reserves," Jerusalem, Israel: The Jerusalem Center for

Public Affairs, April 4, 2013, available from *jcpa.org/article/the-geopolitics-of-israels-offshore-gas-reserves/*.

29. "Egypt Struggles with Gas Supply Challenge," *Middle East Economic Survey*, Issue 56, Vol. 7, February 15, 2013; Ali Aissaoui, "Between a Rock and a Hard Place: Egypt's New Natural Gas Supply Policy," *APICORP Economic Comment*, Vol. 8, No. 3, March 2013.

30. Matt Bradley and Joshua Mitnick, "Egypt Cancels Israel Supply Deal," *The Wall Street Journal*, April 22, 2012. Egypt's reasons to cancel the existing supply contract may indeed be multiple, including Egypt's own increasing domestic gas shortage, exacerbated by a variety of export commitments and the reportedly unattractive gas price negotiated by the Mubarak regime with its Israeli (and Jordanian) customers. This price was tied to the political-ideological opposition of the newly elected Muslim Brotherhood government, which likely saw Israel as the likely first target of export contract revisions, to be later followed up by a doubling of prices for Jordan. See also "Egypt's Gas Exports to Jordan Hit by Domestic Demand 'Crisis'," *LNG Intelligence*, February 6, 2013; "Al-ghaz al-masri muntaqa an al-urdun mundhu 5 ashhar" ("Egyptian Gas to Jordan Interrupted for the Fifth Month"), *Alarab Alyawm*, January 22, 2014.

31. Shoshanna Solomon and Gwen Ackerman, "Israel Starts Tamar Gas Production," *Bloomberg*, May 31, 2013. See also "Let There Be Light?" *LNG Intelligence*, July 12, 2012.

32. It should be noted that Jordan, an Arab country, was also severely hit by Egyptian gas infrastructure attacks and subsequent shortfalls in supply. Unlike with Israel, Egypt offered Jordan a new contract arrangement, which more than doubled the price Jordan had to pay for Egyptian gas virtually overnight, with continued supply disruptions since. Egyptian problems to deliver by now also reflect domestic production shortfalls inside Egypt, primarily as a result to poor planning by the previous Mubarak regime, the vast fiscal deficit amounted as a result of more than 3 years of political paralysis, and subsequent underinvestment in the development of new resources. For example, see "Jordan: First Review Under the Stand-By Arrangement, Request for Waivers of Nonobservance of Performance Criteria, Modification of Perfor-

mance Criteria, and Rephasing of Access—Staff Report," Washington, DC: International Monetary Fund; "Press Release on the Executive Board Discussion; and Statement by the Executive Director for Jordan," Country Report No. 13/130, Washington DC: International Monetary Fund, May 2013, pp. 4, 8, 16.

33. For example, C. Ben-David, "Israel Awards First License to Drill on Golan Heights to Genie," *Bloomberg*, February 21, 2014.

34. For example, see Simon Henderson, "Energy Discoveries in the Eastern Mediterranean: Source for Cooperation or Fuel for Tension? The Case of Israel," *Policy Brief*, Washington, DC: The German Marshall Fund of the United States, June 2012; Tullio Scovazzi, "Maritime Boundaries in the Eastern Mediterranean Sea," *Policy Brief*, Washington, DC: The German Marshall Fund of the United States, June 2012; Eduard Gismatullin, "Israel-Cyprus Deal on Gas as Lebanon Won't Negotiate," *Bloomberg*, April 19, 2012; Amiram Barkat, "Israel Rejects Lebanon EEZ Compromise," *Globes*, October 29, 2013. See also the Arab press, "Kharitat ghaz al-amrikiyyah lil-tawassut beina lubnan wa israil" ("American Gas Map to Mediate between Lebanon and Israel"), *Albawaba*, December 17, 2012; "Israil tarfudhu al-taswiah al-amrikiyyah lil-hudud al-bahriyyah: al-ghaz li" ("Israel Rejects American Mediation for Land Border: Gas"), *Al-Akhbar*, October 31, 2013.

35. The approximate geographical location of Lebanon's offshore blocks is available from Spectrum, the Norwegian company tasked by Lebanon to carry out initial seismic work in its offshore territory. Available from Spectrum's website, *www.spectrumasa.com/press-release/spectrum-extends-lebanon-3d-multi-client-seismic-coverage*.

36. "Landau Says Israel Willing to Use Force to Protect Gas Finds Off Coast," *Bloomberg*, June 24, 2010. See also "Natural Gas Could Lead to New Lebanon-Israel War," *Associated Press*, July 28, 2010.

37. *Ibid.*

38. "Cyprus, Lebanon to Explore Closer Energy Ties," *LNG Intelligence*, January 9, 2013; "Cyprus And Lebanon Discuss Lebanon-Israel Maritime Dispute," *Middle East Economic Survey*, Issue 55, Vol. 13, March 26, 2012.

39. Matthew Bryza, "'Israel-Turkey Pipeline Can Fix Eastern Mediterranean," *Bloomberg*, January 20, 2014.

40. For a background to the Cyprus conflict, see, for instance, Vincent Morelli, "Cyprus: Reunification Proving Elusive," *Congressional Research Service (CRS) Report for Congress*, Washington, DC: CRS, June 25, 2013, available from *www.fas.org/sgp/crs/row/R41136.pdf*; Derya Beyatlı, Katerina Papadopoulou, and Erol Kaymak, "Solving the Cyprus Problem: Hopes and Fears," *Interpeace*, A report produced as part of Cyprus 2015 Initiative, 2011, available from *www.interpeace.org/publications/cyprus/22-solving-the-cyprus-problem-hopes-and-fears-english/file*. "The Cyprus Stalemate: What Next?" *Europe Report No. 171*, Washington, DC: International Crisis Group, March 8, 2006.

41. Part of the considerations is the necessity to ensure Cypriot gas export revenues, in the absence of a comprehensive settlement between the two Cypriot communities, are not simply absorbed by general government spending by the Cypriot state. Provisions such as a Turk-Cypriot heritage fund to benefit Turkish Cypriots once a peace agreement is signed has been one of several propositions. For example, see Toula Onoufriou, "Cyprus—a Future Energy Hub?" Policy Brief, Washington, DC. The German Marshall Fund of the United States, October 2012. See also "Use of Cypriot Gas Deposits as Collateral Premature, Says Kassinis," *Middle East Economic Survey*, Issue 55, Vol. 52, December 21, 2012.

42. "TPAO Begins Drilling Well in Northern Cyprus," *Middle East Economic Survey*, Issue 55, Vol. 19, May 7, 2012.

43. Press Release No. 181 regarding the "Greek Cypriot Administration's Gas Exploration Activities in the Eastern Mediterranean," August 5, 2011, available from *www.mfa.gov.tr*, as quoted in "Aphrodite's Gift: Can Cypriot Gas Power a New Dialogue?" *Europe Report No. 216*, Washington DC: International Crisis Group, April 2, 2012.

44. Press Release No. 43, "Regarding the Second International Tender for Off-Shore Hydrocarbon Exploration Called by the Greek Cypriot Administration (GCA)," February 15, 2012, available from *www.mfa.gov.tr/no_-43_-15-february-2012_-second-international-*

tender-for-off_shore-hydrocarbon-exploration-called-by-the-greek-cypriot-administration-_gca_.en.mfa.

45. "Aphrodite's Gift," International Crisis Group, p. 5.

46. Darbouche, El-Katiri, and Fattouh, p. 7.

47. "Aphrodite's Gift," International Crisis Group, p. 6.

48. Giamouridis, "Natural Gas in Cyprus," p. 7.

49. "Cyprus Energy Ministry Plans Roadmap for Hydrocarbon Industry Launch," *Platts Commodity News*, April 26, 2013.

50. "Cyprus LNG Plans Wobble," *Middle East Economic Survey*, Issue 56, Vol. 41, October 11, 2011.

51. For a background to Turkey's own political turmoil in 2013, see Jim Zanotti, "Turkey: Background and U.S. Relations," *CSR Report for Congress*, Washington, DC: CRS, March 27, 2014, available from *www.fas.org/sgp/crs/mideast/R41368.pdf.*

52. The number of registered Syrian refugees can be accessed via the UNHCR website available from *https://data.unhcr.org/syrianrefugees/regional.php.*

53. "Obama: Chemical Weapons in Syria Are a 'Red Line'," *CBS News*, August 20, 2012. For an overview of the U.S. response to the Syria crisis, see Christopher M. Blanchard *et al.* "Armed Conflict in Syria: Overview and U.S. Response," CRS Report, Washington, DC: CRS, January 15, 2014, available from *www.fas.org/sgp/crs/mideast/RL33487.pdf.*

54. E.g., "Political Infighting Over Oil and Gas Illustrates Lebanese's Electoral Folly," *The National*, October 14, 2013. See also Bassam Fattouh, and Laura El-Katiri, "Lebanon: The Next East Mediterranean Gas Province?" *Oxford Energy Forum*, August 2013, pp. 24-25.

55. "Formation of Lebanon Panel Paves Way for Bid Round," *International Oil Daily*, November 12, 2012.

56. "Political Stalemate Scaring Off Oil Bidders," *The Daily Star*, August 15, 2013; "Lil-marrah al-thalithah: lubnan yumaddi-du muhlah taqdim 'urudh tanqib al-ghaz" ("For the Third Time: Lebanon Extends the Deadline for Gas Exploration Tender"), *Al-Iqtisadiyyah*, January 9, 2014.

57. See Jonathan Stern and Howard Rogers, "The Transition to Hub-Based Gas Pricing in Continental Europe," Jonathan Stern, ed., *The Pricing of Internationally Traded Gas*, Oxford, UK: Oxford University Press, 2012; Jonathan Stern and Howard Rogers, "The Transition to Hub-Based Gas Pricing in Continental Europe," *OIES Working Paper NG49*, March 21, 2011, available from *www.oxfordenergy.org/2011/03/the-transition-to-hub-based-gas-pricing-in-continental-europe/*; Jonathan Stern, "Continental European Long-Term Gas Contracts: Is a Transition Away from Oil Product-Linked Pricing Inevitable and Imminent," *OIES Working Paper NG34*, September 1, 2009, available from *www.oxfordenergy.org/2009/09/continental-european-long-term-gas-contracts-is-a-transition-away-from-oil-product-linked-pricing-inevitable-and-imminent/*.

58. For a discussion of the pros and cons surrounding a direct pipeline from Cyprus to Turkey, see Giamouridis, "Natural Gas in Cyprus," p. 16.

59. A graphically illustrated overview of different Israeli export options can be found at Katie Carnie *et al.*, "Options for Exporting Israeli Gas," *Financial Times*, November 6, 2013, available from *www.ft.com/cms/s/0/b62ba372-463c-11e3-9487-00144feabdc0.html#axzz2rzd7OQwg*.

60. Cyprus has signed Memoranda of Understanding (MOU) with the development consortia of three of its tendered-out blocks in June and November 2013 and has established a time schedule for the construction and beginning of production of an liquefied natural gas liquefaction facility at Vassilikos port, expandable in the future for further production. "Cyprus signs MOU for LNG terminal talks with Noble, Avner, Delek," *Reuters*, June 26, 2013; "Cyprus, Total sign MoU for LNG terminal," *Reuters*, November 7, 2013.

61. "Aphrodite's Gift," International Crisis Group, p. 6.

62. John Reed and Daniel Dombey, "Producers Eye Export Routes for Israeli Gas," *Financial Times*, March 11, 2013.

63. Darbouche, El-Katiri, and Fattouh, pp. 20-23.

64. With relatively little international experience in the application of FLNG, an additional risk to be born is technology risk.

65. See J. Stern *et al.*, "European Alternatives to Russian Gas," OIES Research Paper, Oxford, UK: Oxford Institute for Energy Studies, forthcoming, 2014.

66. Sharon Wrobel and Jonathan Ferziger, "Palestine Power to Pay $1.2 Billion for Gas from Leviathan Well," *Bloomberg*, January 5, 2014; "Palestinians to be First Buyers of Israeli Natural Gas," *The Times of Israel*, January 6, 2014.

67. "Leviathan Signs Initial Deal to Supply Egypt LNG," *Argus*, June 30, 2014; "Israel's Pipeline Hopes," *International Gas Report*, Issue 753, July 14, 2014, p. 10.

68. David Kashi, "Forget John Kerry's Shuttle Diplomacy; Israel and Palestinians Sign Historic Energy Deal," *International Business Times*, January 7, 2014.

69. Egypt, the only other regional gas producer with geographical access to the Gaza Strip though not the West Bank, has been experiencing its own gas shortages due to fast domestic demand growth, struggling to fulfill existing export contracts, and therefore offering no commercial supply option to the Palestinians under current market circumstance. See also Endnote 28.

70. For an overview of the two countries' domestic energy sectors, see *Egypt Country Analysis Brief*, Washington, DC: EIA, July 31, 2013, available from *www.eia.gov/countries/cab.cfm?fips=EG*; and *Jordan Country Analysis Note*, Washington, DC: EIA, available from *www.eia.gov/countries/country-data.cfm?fips=JO*.

71. "Israel-Jordan Sign $500 Million Natural Gas Deal," *The Times of Israel*, February 19, 2014.

72. "Gulf States Finalize Rescue Package For Egypt," *Middle East Economic Survey*, Issue 56, Vol. 28, July 12, 2013; "Egypt Receives Gulf Aid But Qatar Backs Off," *Middle East Economic Survey*, Issue 56, Vol. 39, September 27, 2013; "Saudi-Egypt Power Link Deal Signed, but GCC Grid Usage 'Minimal'," *Middle East Economic Survey*, Issue 56, Vol. 23, June 7, 2013.

73. Simon Henderson, "Natural Gas Export Options for Israel and Cyprus," *Mediterranean Paper Series*, Washington, DC: The German Marshall Fund of the United States, September 2013.

74. "Noble Energy Prefers Selling Leviathan Gas Regionally," *Globes*, November 24, 2013.

75. Various Jordanian news sources suggest Israeli-Jordanian talks have been at a very advanced stage at the time of this writing. For example, "Mubahathat sirriyyah 'al-urduniyyah-al-israiliyyah' bi-sha'n al-ghaz," ("Jordanian-Israeli Secret Talks on Gas"), *Al-'arab al-yaum*, January 9, 2014.

76. Jeremy M. Sharp, "Jordan: Background and U.S. Relations," *CSR Report for Congress*, Washington, DC: CRS, January 27, 2014, available from *www.fas.org/sgp/crs/mideast/RL33546.pdf*.

77. "Ihtidjadjat thid al-hukumah al-misriyyah bisabab tasdir al-ghaz li-isra'il" ("Protest against the Government because of Gas Export to Israel"), *Al-Jazeera*, December 17, 2008; "Khiar al-tadwil aqdiyyah tasdir al-ghaz al-masriy li-isra'il" ("Option of Internationalization of the Exporting Egyptian Gas to Israel"), *Al-Jazeera*, November 21, 2008.

78. Sharp, p. 7.

79. Michael Ratner *et al.*, "Europe's Energy Security: Options and Challenges to Natural Gas Supply Diversification," CRS Report for Congress, Washington, DC: CRS, August 20, 2013, available from *www.fas.org/sgp/crs/row/R42405.pdf*; Kristin Linke and Marcel Vietor, "Beyond Turkey: The EU's Energy Policy and the Southern Corridor," *International Policy Analysis*, Berlin, Germany: Friedrich Ebert Stiftung, November 2010, available from *library.fes.de/pdf-files/id/07553.pdf*. Turkey's energy strategy can also be followed on the Ministry of Foreign Affairs' website: Republic

of Turkey, Ministry of Foreign Affairs, *Turkey's Energy Strategy*, Ankara, Turkey, 2013, available from *www.mfa.gov.tr/turkeys-energy-strategy.en.mfa.*

80. The authors thank one of their friends, who commented on an earlier version of this monograph, for pointing out the wider benefit potential of this "win-win-win" option.

81. See Gulmira Rzayeva, "Gas in the Turkish Energy Market: Policy and Challenges," *Research Paper*, Oxford, UK: Oxford Institute for Energy Studies, February 10, 2014.

82. Matthew Bryza, "An Israel–Turkey Natural Gas Pipeline: Inter-Connection of Commercial and Geopolitical Logic," Oxford Energy Forum, No. 93, August 2013.

83. The UN report outlining the incident is available online. See Geoffrey Palmer *et al*, "*Report of the Secretary-General's Panel of Inquiry on the 31 May 2010 Flotilla Incident*," New York: United Nations, September 2011, available from *graphics8.nytimes.com/packages/pdf/world/Palmer-Committee-Final-report.pdf.*

84. Zanotti, p. 25, referring to a summary of conversation between Netanyahu and Erdogan, from Israeli Prime Minister's Office website, March 22, 2013.

85. For an overview over U.S.-Turkish relations, see *Ibid*.

86. *Ibid.*

87. For example, Masahiro Miyoshi, "The Joint Development of Offshore Oil and Gas in Relation to Maritime Boundary Delimitation," International Boundaries Research Unit (IBRU) *Maritime Briefings*, Vol. 2, No. 5, Durham: University of Durham, 1999.

88. For a background on U.S.-Lebanese and U.S.-Syrian relations, see Christopher M. Blanchard, "Lebanon: Background and U.S. Policy," *CRS Report for Congress*, Washington, DC: CRS, February 14, 2014, available from *www.fas.org/sgp/crs/mideast/R42816.pdf.*

89. Total U.S. foreign aid to Jordan in the financial year 2012 amounted to around $13.1 bn while Egypt, prior to the election of the Muslim Brotherhood government, which was criticized by many Western governments, was in annual receipt of around $1.55 bn U.S. bilateral foreign aid. Sharp, p. 9; Rebecca Nelson, and Jeremy M. Sharp, "Egypt and the IMF: Overview and Issues for Congress," *CRS Report for Congress*, Washington, DC: CRS, April 29, 2013, available from *www.fas.org/sgp/crs/mideast/ R43053.pdf*.

90. Zanotti.

91. U.S. mediation efforts reach back several years ago and were intensified in 2012 and 2013. Barak Ravid, "U.S. Drafts Compromise for Lebanon-Israel Dispute over Natural Gas Resources," *Haaretz*, December 16, 2012; "U.S. Willing to Help Solve Lebanese-Israeli Maritime Border Conflict," *Natural Gas Europe*, July 22, 2013.

www.ingramcontent.com/pod-product-compliance
Lightning Source LLC
Chambersburg PA
CBHW071113280526
45787CB00003B/1025